THE GLORY OF KINGS

A Philosophical Defense of Christianity

By

Larry Hunt

The Eastern Gate Press

Second Edition

Library of Congress Cataloging-in-Publication Data

Hunt, Larry.
The Glory of Kings/Larry Hunt
ISBN: 978-0-615-76882-3

Printed in the United States of America by
The Eastern Gate Press

Cover art: *Awake, O Sleeper!* Larry Hunt

To Sophia,
To seek out a matter is also the glory of queens.

Preliminary Note

My hope for *The Glory of Kings* is both to entertain its readers and to provide them with some fundamental reasons for accepting the claims of Christianity. It does not present a comprehensive defense of the Christian faith but rather a selection of certain philosophical arguments which I think are central to the teachings of Christ and which fit the thematic design of the narrative as a whole. This narrative and the dialogues between its characters are the vehicles through which readers encounter the philosophical arguments. In its essence, then, the book is a work of fiction; nevertheless, its characters quite frequently reference the work of other authors in a way that would require citation in academic research. Therefore, to satisfy my scholastic impulse and the curiosity of readers who might like to track down these references, I have included them as endnotes. If this seems too distracting or pedantic, please just ignore them.

God bless you.

Larry Hunt

"A little philosophy inclineth a man's mind to atheism; but depth in philosophy bringeth man's mind about to religion."

-Sir Francis Bacon, Essays

CONTENTS

One

I was alone on the beach, and it was night. No sound came to my ears but the slow, steady pulsing of the surf and the faint whisper of high grass in the dunes behind me. I forget how long I had lain on that beach, but the sunset (which had purged the heavens with such gold and ruby embers as I will never forget) must have been many hours past. Nevertheless, my will remained firm. I was on a quest, and I had resolved to keep vigil at that spot and not fall asleep until I had achieved the quest. On both sides of me, and pillowed under my head, lay what I thought might be useful tools for the endeavor: Plato's *Dialogues*, an overdue library copy of Wolfram von Eschenbach's *Parzifal*, and, upon my chest, the Bible. There were others as well, works such as *Revelations of Divine Love*, *The City of God*, *Summa Theologica*, *The Journey of the Mind to God*, *The Bhagavad Gita*, *Chuang*

Tzu, an anthology entitled *Classics of Romanticism*, and many more.   But all lay forgotten.   My mind was exhausted, and I was no nearer to the accomplishment of my desire.

Suddenly, a single shooting star fell brightly through the sky. It reminded me of something I had read earlier. "The heavens themselves blaze forth the death of kings,"[i] I mumbled aloud to myself. Where had I read that? I searched my thoughts wearily for the reference, but I soon forgot what I was doing.

I remember thinking that there could be no better place to observe the stars than by the sea. The vastness and unimaginable depth of the clear night sky seemed enhanced by the constant undulations of the wide sea, glimmering and dark. Every distant star in the heavens and every wave striding from the remote horizon to wash upon the sand began to impress me with just how small and alone I really was. I closed my eyes to pray, but no coherent words formed themselves in the murk of my sleepy brain. One thought washed upon another, and that upon another, and that upon another, until I felt myself dreaming and had to shake myself awake. I stood and stretched and gazed again upon the sea.

It was then that I noticed a small object far out among the waves. Steadily, it grew larger, as if it were approaching the shore, but I still had difficulty distinguishing it from the water. Before long I could discern the object's whiteness in the shimmering moonlight; it was clearly moving toward land, though much quicker than the tide should have brought it. I watched intently for several minutes. Then a sudden thrill of shock and disbelief stopped my breath. It was a man, and he was *walking* across the water!

At first I could only see the motion of his arms and legs. His head and body were obscured by what I took to be a garment. As he drew closer, however, I could see that it was not a garment at all but rather his own hair. Long white hair streamed from his head, whipping all about his body like a living cloud as the coastal winds stirred it. Each long stride he made upon the water brought him closer to me, until very soon he drew near the shore and set his bare feet, which were like fine brass, upon the sand just a few yards in front of me.

He stood silently, not moving. A great beard swept down to his shins and was divided into seven braids. His hair, like his beard, was white as freshly washed lamb's wool, or the lofty snows of Mont Blanc, and trails of it still blew in the breeze. It reached to his ankles, covering his entire body and acting as a sort of cloak. His eyes were stars.

"What are you reading?"

At first, the friendliness of his tone was lost on my jolted nerves. I watched him kneel beside the scattered books, quietly examining each of them. After a moment he looked up as if awaiting my answer.

"Oh, uh," I started. "These are some books I'm reading. I'm looking for something."

"What are you looking for?"

Strangely, I found it very difficult to articulate the nature of my quest in his presence.

"Are you looking for God?" he asked.

"Yes," I answered simply.

"Good," he said, returning his attention thoughtfully to the books.

His gentle manner gave me the confidence to venture a question. "Who are you?" I asked.

He looked up again and smiled. It was a forgiving but slightly disappointed smile, the smile of one who had hoped to be recognized without introduction. He stood up, brushing the sand from his knees and hair. "You may call me Amicus, if you like," he said. "But now we should begin.   The impulse to reason is instinctive; therefore, 'come now, and let us reason together.'"[ii] And with that, Amicus strode past me toward the dunes, motioning that I should follow.

I did.

The area of the dunes was relatively short, and he did not speak as he led me across it. He seemed intent on reaching a line of old oak trees marking the edge of the forest through which I had come earlier in the day on my way to the beach. Not until we were under the shadow of their limbs did he again break the silence.

"Do you know All?" he asked.

"What?" I responded. "All of what?"

"Everything. Do you know everything?"

That's a curious question, I thought, but he seemed quite sincere. "No," I said.

He nodded. "Then, do you know anything?"

Though you may laugh to hear it, this very thought had been troubling me earlier. "I'm not sure," I confessed.

"Do you *know* that you are not sure?" he grinned.

I saw that it would be absurd to doubt my own doubt, and I found myself grinning back at him.   "I suppose I do."

"Good. I will tell you two more things that you already know, both of which are necessary for the achievement of your quest. The first is that you know you exist. Do you not remember reading this in the book by Descartes? Something must exist before it can do anything, and doubting is something that you are doing. You doubt; therefore, you are," he laughed.[iii] "The second is that you know Truth exists, Absolute Truth, which is the standard by which all your knowledge is measured. The existence of Absolute Truth is self-evident. He who denies the existence of truth concedes its existence in the very denial, for if there is no truth, then the proposition TRUTH DOES NOT EXIST must itself be true; and if anything is true, truth must exist.[iv] Rest assured, then. You can know some things.   Indeed, self-evident knowledge is so irrefutably true that you are intellectually compelled to believe it once you understand the terms of its propositions. Why did you ever doubt that you could know anything?"

"I was thinking about the definitions of words," I said. "And that led me to the word 'to define.'"

"And what does it mean 'to define'?" he asked.

"To define," I started, hoping to impress him, "comes from the Latin *definire* (*de-*, off + *finis*, end or boundary), a fourth conjugation verb which means to set bounds to; thus, to define something is, conceptually, to encompass it entirely. But in order to do this, I must have absolute knowledge of the thing I am defining. I must be omniscient."

"Are you saying that your definition of 'to define' has taught you that you cannot define anything?"

Sensing that I had slipped into absurdity once again, I did not answer right away. We both stopped walking, and he waited patiently for me as I considered his question. I saw now that we had left the forest path and were surrounded by massive live oaks, all hung with moonlit beards of Spanish moss that wafted in the cool night wind.

Then Amicus sat down quietly on the ground and began to draw something with his finger in the earth. When I leaned nearer to see by the dim moonlight, this is what he had drawn:

$$A \bullet\!\!-\!\!\!-\!\!\!-\!\!\!-\!\!\!-\!\!\!-\!\!\!-\!\!\bullet \Omega$$

"Here are two points, Alpha and Omega," he said. "They set bounds to the line segment between them. Can you step from one point to the other?"

The two points were no more than a foot apart, so I said that I could very easily step from one to the other.

"Show me," he said.

I did.

"Good," he nodded. "Now you see that it can be done. How long would you say it took to make the journey?"

"From Alpha to Omega? I don't know, a second maybe."

Again, he nodded. "Now, when you moved from one point to the other, did you pass through this middle point?" he asked, pushing his finger into the soil in the middle of the line segment he had drawn.

"Yes," I said.

"And this point, did you pass through this point as well?" he asked, making another point half-way between the middle point and the Alpha point.

"Yes, certainly," I answered.

"And this one?" he asked again, making yet another point in the same manner.

"Yes," I said. "I passed through all the points between Alpha and Omega."

"And how many points are there between Alpha and Omega?" he asked.

Suddenly I saw his point, so to speak. "An infinite number," I said.

He smiled. "And what is the definition of 'infinite'?"

"'Infinite' comes from the Latin *infinitus* (*in-*, without or not + *finis*, end or boundary), an adjective which means without an end or boundary."

"How long should it take to move through an infinite number of points?"

"An unending amount of time," I responded.[v]

"But you remember that it took only a second, right?"

"Yes."

"Thus, you see that the finite can contain the infinite, though you cannot understand how. It is the same with words; indeed, it is the same with The Word. Words set bounds to infinity and make that which is infinite comprehensible to your finite mind, though you cannot understand how they do these things. This is why your definition of 'to define' can teach you that you cannot define something in an absolute sense. You are right to say that you do not have All Knowledge. You cannot hope to know something absolutely, as God does. Only the Creator, who sets the very borders of his creature's existence, knows that creature's absolute definition. You, whose mind is bound by time and space, must content yourself with signs and symbols of Truth, frail metaphors that often break in the hands of too eager philosophers. This is why the proverb says, 'Lean not on your own understanding.'"[vi]

"But what other choice do I have?" I protested. "I *must* lean on my own understanding. Even if I decide to put my trust in something outside myself, it is my own understanding that leads me to that decision."

"The proverb does not tell you to renounce your capacity for reason. It tells you that this capacity for reason is wholly insufficient by itself. You have seen this just now in the paradox of the line segment. But reason is a divine gift, and as such it can help you find knowledge. Remember that there are also other proverbs. These proverbs assume that it is possible for you to gain knowledge of the truth in spite of the fact that you are not omniscient. 'Wisdom is the principal thing; therefore get wisdom. Exalt her, and she will promote you. She will place on your head an ornament of grace; a crown of glory she will deliver to you.'[vii] All true philosophers know that the love of wisdom is well requited. But come; I will show you more clearly."

He reached out, and, with the faintest touch of his finger to my temple, brought deep sleep over me like fragrant oil moving down slowly over my head.

Two

When I awoke, it was daytime. Sunlight filtered through the leaves and moss-hung limbs of the oak forest, and I lay in the sandy crossroads at the center of the island. Amicus sat beside me. I saw that he was writing again with his finger in the soil, so I sat up and looked. This is what he wrote.

MERCY IS A KIND OF SORROW.

M) S

SORROW IS AN IMPERFECTION.

S) ~P

THEREFORE MERCY IS AN IMPERFECTION.

∴ M) ~P

GOD IS PERFECT.

G) P

THEREFORE GOD IS NOT MERCIFUL.

∴ G) ~M

viii

———————————————

LOVE IS MERCIFUL.

L) M

GOD IS LOVE.

G) L

THEREFORE GOD IS MERCIFUL.

∴ G) M

When he finished writing these things, he looked over at me. "Consider these two arguments," he said. "Are they both valid deductions?"

"Yes," I answered, studying them closely.

"Then why do their conclusions contradict each other?" he asked.

"Because they follow from different premises," I responded.

"Yes, depending upon what premises you accept, it is possible to prove two completely exclusive and contradictory ideas."

"So how am I supposed to know which premises to accept?"

His answer baffled me at first, for it was in a strange language, filled with soft snorts and grunts. Only when I heard the gentle tread of hooves in the sand behind me did I realize that he was not addressing me. I turned and saw one of the island's wild horses standing over me.

On an impulse, I stood up and slid onto the animal's bare back, and she accepted me as naturally as if she were a part of me. Leaning forward, I patted her muscular neck and scratched her hairy ears admiringly. "What is her name?" I asked.

"Her name is Reason," said Amicus.

"She is beautiful," I said.

"Yes," he agreed as he stood and reached out to stroke her velvety nostrils. "And now you must ride her to the sea. Which of these four roads will you take?" he asked.

I looked at the north road, the south, the west, and the east, pondering which would be best. "Does it matter which one I choose?"

"Very much," he answered.

"But this is an island. They all lead to the sea," I retorted.

"Do both of these arguments lead to a valid conclusion?" he asked, indicating what he had written in the ground at his feet.

"Yes."

"Are the consequences of following one path of Reason equal to those of following another?"

"No," I confessed.

"Then your decision about which path to take is very important."

Seeing that he was right, I considered each path once more. "Would you help me decide?" I asked.

"Certainly. You should take the east road," he said, pointing in that direction. As soon as he did this, he began to walk down that road.

It was not the road that I would have picked, but I trusted his judgment and did not want to be separated from him, so I rode Reason after him under the dappled light of the overarching branches which sheltered the eastern road. Before long, the coastal winds were stirring around us again, and we emerged into the brightness of the beach. We continued walking over the dunes right down onto the smooth, wet sand until finally Reason felt the wash of surf swirling around her hooves, and she stopped.

Here Amicus spoke again. "Reason can carry you this far," he noted, "but your goal is farther off than these shores." With this, he gestured toward the sea, whose undulations stretched on into the incalculable distance. "You must journey on this, the Deep, the Abyss. It is Death, and you must cross it."

I looked upon it and shuddered. "Why?" I asked.

"Because that is the only way to knowledge and life," he said.

"How am I to do it?"

"Behold," he said.

Somehow I had missed it before, but there, moored just off shore, was an odd looking ship. The length of it was three hundred cubits, the height, thirty cubits, and the breadth must have been fifty cubits. It had three stories, a window, and a door. Its name was inscribed with gold letters on its side: FAITH.

"Come inside with me," Amicus said, and I followed him into the ship where he closed the door behind us. Then he led me to the window, grabbing it with his powerful hands and throwing it open. The island of Reason was lost to sight now as I thrust my head out into the salt air. All around was only the Deep, and it lapped hungrily at the gopher wood planks of the sturdy vessel.

"Look there," Amicus said, pointing out of the window toward the east, the direction in which we were heading. I followed his gaze and saw, blazing in unspeakable glory, the brilliant face of the sun as it shone in eternal splendor above the eastern horizon.

"That is the One for whom you are looking, He Who Is, The Absolute, The Ancient of Days, who sits forever on The Mercy Seat," said Amicus solemnly.

"But how can we reach *that?*" I asked incredulously.

"By faith," he answered.

"What is faith?" I asked.

"Faith is an act of the will; it is informed by reason but extends beyond the reach of reason. You are not required to understand with your own understanding how a ship can sail to the sun. You are only required to set sail. God will see to the rest. Coleridge says it well. Perhaps you remember? 'The scheme of Christianity, though not discoverable by human reason, is yet in accordance with it; that link follows link by necessary consequence; that religion passes out of the ken of reason only where the eye of reason has reached its own horizon; and that faith is then but its continuation.'"[ix]

Even as he spoke the words, I did, in fact, remember reading them earlier, but then another thought occurred to me. "What would have happened," I ventured, "if I had ridden Reason down one of the three other roads? "

"You would have come to the shore and found another boat of the same name but of different make and proportions. If you had taken that boat, it would have sunk into the Deep with you."

Again, I shuddered.

He put his hand on my shoulder reassuringly. "It is the same with everyone, you know," he said.

"You mean even unbelievers have faith?" I asked.

"Everyone has faith, but not everyone has faith in what is trustworthy," he said. "If the home of Reason were large enough to reach Truth, then you could simply ride straight there, provided you took the correct path. But her home is not so large; it is a tiny island in the midst of the Deep. There is no land, nothing solid between Reason and the Absolute, except Faith, to which Reason leads you."

I leaned out the window and looked to the Bright East. "If the existence of Truth, of Absolute Truth, is self-evident, then shouldn't the existence of God also be self-evident?" I asked. "God is Truth itself. As Christ says, 'I am the way, *the truth*, and the life.'[x] Therefore, the proposition 'God exists' should be self-evident."

"Aquinas answers himself on this point," Amicus replied. "Remember? One cannot imagine the opposite of a proposition which is self-evident. But every fool who says in his heart, 'There is no God' imagines the opposite of the proposition 'God is.' Therefore, God's existence is not self-evident.[xi] When you say that God is Truth, you are speaking poetically. It is one of those fragile metaphors that can break in the hands of too eager philosophers. For instance, I might say of a strong man, 'He is an ox,' but to conclude from this statement that the man has horns is to misunderstand the meaning of the metaphor. God is more than just another true thing. He is the root of all true things (to use another metaphor). This is what the proposition 'God is Truth' asserts, but God is also more than the abstracted concept of truth. He is a Person with a Mind, the omniscient and loving Creator of Everything."

"But why isn't his existence self-evident?" I asked, turning to look at Amicus, who leaned out the window beside me. "Of all things that ought to be self-evident, I would have thought that the existence of the Creator of Everything ought to be one of them. God could have made his own existence self-evident to me if he had wanted to."

"I agree. So what do you conclude from that?" Amicus asked.

"That he did not want to," I said.

Amicus confirmed my conclusion with a nod.

"But why wouldn't he want to?" I persisted.

He did not answer. He merely gazed out toward the East and let the winds of the open sea blow peacefully upon his face. I sighed but did not ask the question again. Instead, I mimicked his own actions and looked eastward in silence.

Eventually, however, I became distracted by the rhythmic slap of the waves against the sides of our ship, and I looked down to watch them. Ceaselessly, they rocked the boat and curled their lolling crests around its bow with a hypnotist's monotony. After only a few minutes of being absorbed in the enchantment of their movement, my head dropped suddenly with drowsiness. I blinked in surprise. It was odd that I should be sleepy, having just woken up only a little while earlier. But I was very sleepy. Perhaps if I just rested a minute it would pass, I thought, and so I sat on the floor and leaned my head back against the wooden wall.

"Come with me," Amicus said kindly, noticing my weariness. I arose and followed him to the innermost room of the ship. And behold, I saw a very fair bed upon which lay a crown of silk.[xii] "Rest here," he said, indicating the bed. Then I lay down and slept.

Three

The next thing that I recall is resting on my back, eyes closed, upon a cold outcrop of rock.

"Are you ready to continue?" I heard Amicus ask.

I opened my eyes, and there he sat, smiling his kindly smile. "Yes," I replied, sitting up.

"Good," he said.

I looked all around me, noticing for the first time where I was. We both sat at the very summit of a lofty mountain, higher than all the surrounding mountains. Deep drifts of snow claimed every inch of the serene landscape except for the pinnacle of rock that served as our seat. On one side, the mountain dropped sharply into a ravine whose bottom was hidden by clouds that floated below us. The other side was passable, but I did not see any footprints in the snow.

"How would you define free will?" my teacher asked.

I thought for a moment. "Free will is the ability to cause one's own actions, to act without being caused to act by anything beyond oneself, to choose to act in a particular way."

He nodded. "Do you believe that some things have free will?"

I hesitated, for this was another point that I had been debating with myself for some time. "I'm not sure," I finally admitted.

"You know," Amicus laughed softly, "nobody is intellectually compelled to deny the possibility of free will."

I laughed too, hoping that he would notice my appreciation of the irony in his statement.

"As for those who choose not to believe that they have the power to choose," he said gently, "Dante has accurately described them. They have lost the good of the intellect.[xiii] Those who choose to reject the possibility of free will must find themselves forced into the absurd position of believing that their very real capacity for knowledge, for being conscious of truth, is inexplicable."

"What do you mean?"

"Behold," he said, reaching down. He picked up a stone and held it for a moment before letting it drop into his other hand. "How much knowledge did this stone need to fall as it did?"

"None," I said.

"How much knowledge would you need to fall in exactly the same way if you were dropped from the summit of this great mountain?"

I looked out at the high peaks below our mountain and at the drifting clouds and distant gulfs below those peaks. "None," I answered.

"So, knowledge does not help you to fall?"

I shook my head.

"And if you were dropped, would the knowledge that you were falling help you to stop falling if you desired to stop?"

"No, because there would be nothing I could do about it. I would have no choice but to fall. Something other than me would be causing me to fall."

"Then knowledge does not help you *not* to fall either," he concluded. "But the capacity for knowledge suggests an accompanying capacity for choice. If nothing ever caused its own actions, then knowledge would be as unnecessary and useless in every action as it is in the act of falling, and your capacity to learn and reason and know, while undeniable, would be absurd and inexplicable. "

"Yes," I said, seeing his point. "There would be no explaining it. How could we? Even the theory of evolution couldn't explain it. Evolution claims that the faculties we possess now have been useful for survival in the past, but if our will is not free to cause any of our actions, then how has knowledge, the consciousness of information ever been useful? Why would my conscious mind be informed of anything if that mind does not have the ability to choose one act rather than another in at least some scenarios?"

"Now then," Amicus continued, "why did the stone fall?"

"Gravity acted on it," I replied.

"Do you believe that the first place to look for the cause of a thing's actions should be the thing itself or some other thing?"

"The thing itself. That would be the best starting point because it is the simplest explanation. As William of Ockham says, needlessly complicating an explanation is unjustifiable and only increases the likelihood of error." [xiv]

"Then why did you look for something beyond the stone itself to explain its actions? Why did you complicate your explanation by positing a second thing called gravity to explain the actions of the stone?"

"Well," I said, trying to retrace my thoughts, "I suppose I did that because I thought that that particular complication was necessary to explain the stone's actions. One should only look for a second thing to explain the actions of the first if one concludes that the first thing was unable to cause the actions of its own accord. And I don't think a stone can cause any of its own actions."

"Why not?"

"Because being able to cause one's own actions means having free will, which implies having a mind, an *animus*. But the stone is inanimate. It does not have a mind."

"What is gravity?"

"A force, one of the four fundamental forces of nature."

"Does it have a mind?"

"No."

"If you reject the stone itself as the cause of its own actions because it has no mind, then why would you accept gravity or any other mindless force as the ultimate cause of the stone's actions? If gravity is mindless, then it, like the stone, can only act while being acted upon. Should you not assume that a mind (something than *can* act of its own accord) must lie beyond gravity itself in order to explain its actions on the stone?"

"I had not thought of that," I confessed. "But isn't a thing with a mind more complex than a thing without one?"

"This is not the question before us," he corrected me. "You have already accepted that some things have the ability to cause their own actions; thus, you have already accepted that some things either are or have minds. The question before us is this: Is it simpler to believe that a given action was caused by one agent (which could cause its own actions) or by two agents (one which could not cause its own actions and one which could cause its own actions)?"

"I see," I said.

"If someone had not made up his mind about free will," he went on, "and wanted to settle the issue based solely on the simplicity of the scenario, the question would be something like this: Is it simpler to believe that a given action was caused by one agent (which could cause its own actions) or by an infinity of agents (not one of which could cause its own actions) all acting in unison at the same moment in time."

"Why at the same moment in time?"

"Because something that cannot cause its own actions can only act while being acted upon by something else," he answered.

I nodded.

"But let us return to the concept of gravity as a mindless force. Is there anything in gravity's effects that logically disqualifies it from being a mind?"

"Some people might point to gravity's regular, predictable behavior as a sign that it is mindless."

"What does 'regular' mean?" he asked.

"It comes from Latin *regula*, meaning 'rule.' Regular behavior follows a rule."

"You have a mind," he pointed out, "so you know that things with minds create rules and follow rules and enforce rules. Is this not what good parents do? Do they not establish rules for their house and follow and enforce these rules consistently so their children can learn what to expect? A very strong mind could behave with a degree of regularity that might astonish weaker minds, but this regularity would be a symptom of its strength, not of its mindlessness. Therefore, since there is empirical evidence associating regular behavior with minds, it is unreasonable to view regular behavior as a sign of mindlessness."

"But isn't there also empirical evidence of mindless things acting regularly?" I asked. "What about machines?"

"If a machine acts, it does so because it is being acted upon by natural forces, and it is the nature of these forces that is in dispute. You cannot cite a mindless machine's regular behavior as an example of regular behavior in a mindless thing when that behavior is owing to something other than the machine itself, something that might, in fact, be a mind."

I nodded in agreement.

"Since there is no logical impediment to conceiving of gravity as a mind, let us return to Ockham's razor. What would be the simplest explanation for the ability of gravity to act upon the stone? Is it simpler to believe that gravity acts of its own accord, or that it cannot act of its own accord and that something else acts upon it so that it can act upon the stone?"

"It is always simpler to look for the cause of a thing's actions in the thing itself rather than in some other thing, so I suppose it would be simpler to believe that the thing called 'gravity' acts of its own accord. It would be simpler to conceive of it as a mind, which chooses to act."

"Now then," he continued. "You said that there were four such forces?"

"If I remember correctly."

"Should we not apply the same line of reasoning to the other three and conclude that they are also best conceived of as minds?"

"I don't see why we wouldn't."

"Very well. Let us consider these four minds. We have deduced that they must exist in the present moment. But now we must ask how these four minds have come to exist at all. Anything that exists must either always exist, or have come into being at some point in the past."

"Yes," I agreed.

"Let us use Ockham's razor once more. Which is simpler, Being or Coming into Being?"

I thought about it for a moment. "Being," I posited.

"Why?"

"Because Being is only a part of Coming into Being."

Amicus nodded. "Before we learn otherwise, then, what is the simplest explanation for how these four minds have come to exist at the present moment?"

"We should assume that they always are, that they have no beginning since Coming into Being requires a change of state from their present one, and this change would require an additional explanation."

"Yes," Amicus agreed, "but now let us consider what a being that has no beginning must be like," he continued. "Since it has no beginning, it always IS. Such a being must be complete in itself. It must exist in absolute, independent perfection, for if it lacked anything in itself that was necessary for its existence, it would require some other being to supply that need before it could exist."

I nodded my assent.

"How many ways can an absolutely perfect being exist?" Amicus asked.

"Only one," I said, perceiving at last where he was leading me.

"Exactly," he said. "To exist without beginning means to exist in absolute perfection, and yet perfection implies singularity; therefore, all four of these minds cannot exist perfectly. If we say that one of these four minds is perfect, then the other three cannot be perfect since they are different from the one at least in as much as they are not it. Any deviation from perfection is imperfection.[xv] Thus, these other three minds would be incomplete in themselves, requiring the one perfect mind both to bring them into being and to support their existence. Would it not be simpler to conclude, then, that these four minds are really one, and that this one perfect, eternal mind is responsible for the effects that you now attribute to the various mindless forces of nature?"

"I see," I said.

"Good," he smiled.

"So, do you mean that a single, eternal, omniscient and omnipotent mind is the simplest, and therefore most probable, explanation for the universe as we find it?"

"I mean more than that," said my teacher. "I mean not only that it *is* the simplest, but that it has always been and always will be the simplest, and therefore most probable, explanation for the universe as you find it."

"Always *will be?*"

He nodded. "No discovery will ever change that reality. Let us say that one day you conclude, based on empirical evidence, that these forces of nature themselves are mindless entities, unable to act on their own. When you come to this conclusion, you must deduce that something lies beyond the mindless forces to explain their actions just as you deduced that something lay beyond the mindless stone to explain its falling. What, then, will be the simplest explanation for the actions of the forces of nature?"

"A single, eternal mind," I said softly, stunned.

Again, Amicus nodded. "No matter how many mindless forces you discover, no matter how many finite minds, though their native power may be seraphic, you will always be best able to explain their existence by the existence and actions of this one infinite and perfect mind."

Eagerly, I pressed my teacher further. "What else can we infer from the fact that this mind is perfect?" I asked. "Can we know anything about its..." I struggled for the right word, "its personality?"

"Think of the imperfect personalities with whom you are familiar," he suggested. "What essential qualities do those have who are the least imperfect?"

"Those who are the least imperfect are the most virtuous," I said, "those who most often practice love, joy, peace, faith, patience, self-control, and forgiveness."

"These qualities find their perfection in the one perfect being," said Amicus. "You know that being good is the best way to be. Being good is, therefore, synonymous with being this Perfect Being. He is the standard by which all imperfect goodness is measured. You can no more imagine an absolutely perfect being that is cruel, disloyal, and petty than you can imagine a square circle. All minds that come into being, to the degree that they can recognize goodness, are compelled to acknowledge its objective beauty. And all those who recognize its beauty are compelled to acknowledge that they ought to choose to be as good as they possibly can be. In this choice lies the central purpose of all creatures who perceive that beauty."

"What about those creatures that are unable to perceive such beauty? Do they have a purpose in being?" I asked.

Here he paused and looked at me expectantly, but as I did not know what he could be expecting, I neither said nor did anything. After a moment, his patient smile returned, and he held the stone out to me.

I took it.

"All that comes into being is a purposeful creation of the Eternal Mind," he said. "Thus, everything that comes into being has meaning, divine and absolute meaning, even that stone."

My eyes fell to the stone in my hand.

"So," he asked, "what is the divine meaning of the stone?"

"How can I know that?" I asked incredulously.

"Tell me what is true about it," he offered. "When you begin to find out what a thing truly is, you begin to understand its divine meaning. The more you learn about a creation, the more you learn about its purpose in existing."

I shrugged skeptically. "It's rough," I observed, "and solid, and grey, and I can carry it in my hand."

"Try harder," Amicus pushed.

I thought in silence for some time. "I also see that *all* of the actions of the stone are common to all physical bodies, and, therefore, I can conclude that it has no mind that is particular to it. The same mind that determines all of the actions of the stone must also determine all of the actions even of the planets and stars. I suppose, then, that at least part of the purpose of the stone is to bear witness to this mind which absolutely governs all the physical objects of the universe, all those, at least, which have no mind particular to them."

"Good," Amicus approved of my conclusion. "In this way even a mindless stone may cry out in praise of its creator," he smiled, "and the heavens may declare the glory of God."

"And by contrasting my own actions with those of the stone," I continued, encouraged, "I can see that I differ from the stone in that not all of my own actions are common to all physical bodies. Many of them are, maybe most of them are, but not all. So another purpose for the stone's existence must be to make me aware of my own mind, the mind that is particular to me and allows me to act of my own accord." I was so moved by this last observation that a strange feeling of affection for the stone stirred in me, a sense almost of kinship between me and that solid little unconscious ambassador of its maker and mine. I smiled at it and laughed under my breath.

"What are you thinking?" Amicus asked.

In answer, I reverently placed the stone on the ground before me, like one of the ancients beginning an altar to the great I AM. "I would like to leave this stone here, Amicus, on the top of this mountain, as a memorial to your lesson."

"So be it," he said. "And now that you have done so, may we not say something new about this stone's purpose in existing?"

I looked back at the stone where I had set it, puzzled. "What do you mean?"

"The stone is now the medium through which something new has come into being," he said. "A memorial has come into being. And who is its creator?"

"I am."

"Then you have contributed to the definition of the stone by your making of this memorial," he said.

"But I haven't really brought anything into being have I?" I asked. "The stone and the memorial are the same thing."

"Are a poem and the ink in which it is written the same thing?" Amicus responded.

I shook my head.

"Then neither are the memorial and the stone," he concluded. "Something that has never before existed has come into being. But you must not believe that you are the sole creator of this memorial because, in truth, it is only partly your creation."

"You mean God created the stone, but I created the memorial?" I asked.

"No, I mean God created the stone, and he also had a hand in creating the memorial. The I AM dwells in his creations, though he is also distinct from them and superior to them. His relationship to his creation is similar to that of a poet to his poem. Part of a poet dwells within his poem because its very being stems from him, and yet the poet is not the poem. The I AM dwells in you because you are his creation. You can create something entirely new, like this memorial, because the I AM creates within you according to your will.

Whenever you create, you create because the I AM, who dwells within you, creates. This means that your creation will have two meanings particular to it in the minds of its creators (the I AM and you). It will have a divine, absolute meaning, as a creation of the I AM, and a relative one in your own mind, as your own creation. The divine meaning incorporates the relative one but is distinct from it."

"Do you mean to say that each and every creation of humanity has a divine purpose?" I asked, incredulous again.

"Yes," he responded calmly.

"But humans are imperfect and often make evil things. What if I create something evil? Is God in that evil thing? How could *it* have a divine purpose?"

"Did a human create the Cross?"

He allowed me to contemplate this question in silence before finally rising and beckoning for me to follow. "I have more to show you," he said.

I had not noticed it earlier, but a tiny stream issued from a spring in our rock seat, and we rose and followed its frosty path through the ice and snow down the negotiable side of the mountain. As we left, I glanced back at the memorial I had made, and Amicus, seeing me do this, resumed his lesson.

"So, the stone has meaning as a memorial simply because you choose for this to be so in your mind," Amicus said. "There was no need even to change its form; only your imaginative perception of it was necessary. The problem comes in when you no longer recognize the distinction between a thing's divine meaning and the relative meaning, which your own mind gives it. This is rightly called madness."

Something in his tone unsettled me. "Am I in danger of that?" I asked.

"No. You are in danger of something else altogether. Behold," he said, pointing ahead.

I looked, and there I saw a mill that was fed by the little stream we had been walking beside.

"You must experience the mill on your own. I will await your return here beside the stream." And with that he sat down beneath the thick branches of an oak, folded his arms, and nodded his head to indicate that I should proceed.

I started resolutely toward the mill, fearful but determined to pass whatever test it held for me, when, out of its door, stepped a demon clothed in breeches and a dark woolen coat. His face was pale and fleshy, and dark-rimmed eyes of madness looked arrogantly at me from beneath a high round forehead.

"After you," he said, waving me inside. I entered the mill.

After walking for some time, we eventually came upon a cave and descended into its labyrinthine recesses, groping blindly, until a great gulf yawned at our feet. Still feeling our way arduously, we each managed to find a place to sit and thus perched precariously above this abyss, I in a stout, gnarled oak root, and he in a huge mushroom of some sort, which hung upside down beside my root.

But there was light there, faint at first, and slowly our eyes adjusted to it well enough to behold the waves of the Deep below us. The light came from a pervasive, fiery smoke which cast its lurid glimmer over all. And as I looked to the West, a flaming brow burst furiously out of the waters, spewing steam and smoke for miles around. The shape reared immensely out of the black sea until the demon and I both beheld its terrible, globe-like eyes, crimson as the blood that streaked its gaping maw. It was the green and purple striped head of Leviathan. Then the demon spoke.

"Behold," he said, leaning against the stem of his fungus. "All that you see is but a construct of my making," he laughed insipidly. I was not daunted.

"You are mistaken and quite mad," I said confidently. "What is before us is real; if you imagine that its existence is dependent upon your imagination, then you confuse your own imagination with that of God. If all this is, indeed, only a construct of your making, then change it," I challenged.

"Fool! Foolish man!" he laughed and shut his bulging eyes tightly, as if to concentrate harder. When he opened them again, the gleeful anticipation on his face melted into disappointment, and then confusion, for everything remained just as it had been. We still sat perched over the abyss.

"I don't understand," he said weakly.

"Be glad," I said. "You have just escaped from madness by distinguishing between your own creations and those of the I AM."

He thought about this for a moment, and, slowly, his face smoothed. He turned to me and smiled softly.

"Yes," he said quietly. "I believe you are right."

"Good," I said smugly. "After all, 'the man who never alters his opinion is like standing water, and breeds reptiles of the mind.'"[xvi]

Glutted and radiant with success, I climbed back up out of the cave, through the mill, and outside. I could see Amicus still sitting beside the stream under the tree where I had left him. When I approached, he rose to greet me. "Well, how did you find your experience in the mill?" he asked.

"Very satisfying," I laughed, leaning confidently against the trunk of the great tree. "I met with William Blake himself and convinced him that he was wrong."

Amicus acknowledged my report with a nod, but there was a kind of sorrow in his eyes as he did so. "You have learned many useful things," he said. "You have learned that you exist because you are a creation of a the great I AM. And you have learned that your existence, therefore, has divine meaning. But what you have not yet learned is what that meaning is."

"Teach me," I said eagerly. "I would very much like to know."

Then I heard something behind me.

The first sounds of its hooves drumming rapidly upon the earth came faintly to my ears, and I turned around, confused. The beats had seemed quite far off, initially, but by the time I turned to look, the drumming of its hooves had become a thunder which shook the very ground beneath my feet. It was a centaur, black as a Night Mare. With one easy motion she caught me up in her long goblin arms and crushed the wind out of me. I tried desperately to scream for help, but all I could manage was a painful, incoherent gasp.

A wild terror of disbelief seized me. What was happening? I did not dare move, not that I would have been able to if I had dared, so strong was my captor's merciless grip. She tucked me in the crook of her foul arm as easily as I would have carried a book.

I traveled a long while like this. At some point, however, her pace slowed, and as it did I looked up to see a wondrous castle. Its formidable outer wall made a perfect circle of smooth stone and reached so high that only a bird or a leaf upon the wind could have managed to enter its precincts unbidden. No mortal army, however large, could ever have reduced it, and I dreaded to enter those walls, but enter we did. Only after we were in the castle proper did the centaur finally halt before two great doors of steel, which she unbolted and pushed open. Then, without ceremony or explanation, she threw me down, and the doors slammed shut behind me with a terrible boom.

Four

Tentatively I sat up, scanning the room, and found that I was not alone. The room itself appeared to be the castle's great hall. It was dark but for the low fire that burned in the hearth, and there was no furniture of any kind in the room. Its four inhabitants were seated on the floor before the fireplace. One of them, an elderly woman, spoke to me first.

"Why don't you join us?" she asked. Her voice had a disarming and inviting quality about it, so I stirred myself and walked cautiously over to the small group. Hopefully, they could tell me where I was.

Three of the four sat in a loose triangle while the fourth sat closest to the fire, a little apart from the group. This one had a sturdy, muscular build, but he reclined on one elbow as if from overweariness, and a cloak of sable fur lay over his legs and waist for warmth. His eyes were blue and his face was set in a flinty grimace as he regarded me coldly. He wore a knight's tabard.

The woman who had invited me to join the group had gray hair, a gentle face, and the thin, delicate build of an ascetic. Her eyes reminded me of Reason's, though I can't say why.

"My name is Julian," she said and rested her hand lovingly upon the head of the tiny girl who sat beside her, "and this is Autumn." The waif, who seemed about seven years old, grinned at me innocently. She was clothed in a vernal-green dress of Arabian silk and held a stone in her little hands. I was quite surprised to recognize it as the same stone that I had left as a memorial on the summit of Mont Blanc. Noticing my interest in it, Julian explained, "Autumn bears the *lapsit exillis*."[xvii]

Lapsit exillis? Where had I head those words before? They had been in something I was reading earlier….

"My name is Faust," offered a heavy-set man sitting across from Julian and Autumn. He wore a scholar's mortarboard and was clad in rich garments of ermine. Around his neck was a golden chain and amulet with which he was obsessively fiddling. "I am Professor of Philosophy at the University of Wittenburg."

I nodded my thanks to them all and managed an apprehensive smile. Then, I turned to Julian. "Where am I?" I asked. "What is this place?"

"You are in the great hall of Castle Munsalvaesche," she answered.

"But why?"

She paused for a minute, as if unsure of how to answer me.

"I'll tell him," the knight offered wryly.

"Anfortas," Julian said, turning to face him.

He met her look with one of irritated deference. Faust, for his part, sighed and held his head in his hands, massaging his temples as if they hurt or he were tired of thinking.

Julian turned back to me and answered steadily. "You have been condemned to die," she said. "We all have. This is our holding cell until the executioner comes to take us away."

The words struck me like a lance. My body went numb, and my heart began to beat desperately. "What?" I asked weakly. "What did you say?" My mind was reeling in an attempt to reinterpret Julian's words. They couldn't be right.

"You're going to die," Anfortas echoed.

I looked into his pitiless face and recoiled. *What?* I stared at the floor. I was nauseous, and my head felt cold and tingled as the blood drained out of it. Realizing I was about to black out, Julian sent Autumn scurrying to help me sit down. One tiny hand grabbed me and directed my collapse as best it could while the other clutched the *lapsit exillis*. As I sat there on the cold floor, the pronouncement sounded over and over in my mind. *You have been condemned to die.* Why? Was I really going to die? The whole scene seemed unreal to me, almost like a dream, but a dream from which I could not wake. For some time, I was so absorbed in the shock of my fate that I completely lost track of the other people. I even failed to notice little Autumn as she sat beside me, gently stroking my hand. It was the voice of Faust that finally made its way into the numbed recesses of my brain and sparked me to consciousness once again.

"Even if there were such a being as God, a being capable of creating the entire universe with all of the unfathomably great distances between galaxies, the infinitesimal minutiae of quarks, and all the laws that govern our existence, don't you think that this Being would be so superior to us that we could not hope to understand it or communicate with it using our pitiful little minds?"

Anfortas gave a faint laugh. "You don't seem like the sort of man who thinks of his mind as being a little thing," he observed.

Julian tactfully intercepted Faust's reply. "But Johann," she said, "don't you think that a being capable of creating such wonderful things would also be capable of communicating with his creation if he chose to?"

Faust reluctantly conceded the point. "But does he choose to? Perhaps that is the real question," the doctor retorted.

"Always," Julian asserted, "but never more clearly than through Christ himself."

"You are asking too much of me, Julian," Faust protested.

"It is not I who ask it of you," she said gently. "And it is not too much."

"Was Christ a human?" he asked.

"Yes, and God," Julian answered.

"Does he ever actually claim to be God in the Scriptures?"

"The gospel of John begins by calling Christ the Word, and says, 'The Word was God. He was in the beginning with God. All things were made through Him, and without Him nothing was made that was made. In Him was life.'[xviii] Later in that same book, Christ calls himself by God's own name: 'Most assuredly, I say to you, before Abraham was, I AM.'"[xix]

"But humans are finite beings," Faust declared. "We exist in space and time, and God must be infinite. How can what is infinite be contained in what is finite? That is impossible."

Suddenly, I heard Autumn's little voice at my side. Under her breath she was singing a verse from some song, apparently to herself, as she rolled the *lapsit exillis* around playfully in the palm of her hand:

> "To see a World in a Grain of Sand,
>
> And a Heaven in a Wild Flower,
>
> Hold Infinity in the palm of your hand,
>
> And Eternity in an hour...."[xx]

Is this one condemned as well? I asked myself. *Will the executioner come for her too?* A protective urge rippled through me, and I reached out to hug her to my side and comfort her, but as I did I noticed my hands trembling. She looked up at me and smiled, and I wondered who was comforting whom. Suddenly a powerful welling of self-pity arose from deep inside me, and I clutched the child to myself and began to weep. I tried to keep quiet so as not to draw attention to myself, but the intensity of my weeping grew the more I indulged it until eventually my choking gasps intruded upon the debate.

"Julian, why don't you send the children to a corner somewhere?" Anfortas suggested.

Instantly a quiver of rage pierced my body, and I glared fiercely at the knight. He, however, returned my look contemptuously, not showing the slightest alarm at my angry display.

"Leave him alone, Anfortas," Julian said. Then she turned to me. "I know this must be a shock to you. Don't be embarrassed. Are you okay?"

I lied and nodded yes, pulling myself together.

"I can't explain how what is infinite can be contained in what is finite," Julian confessed to Faust. "I follow Christ for other reasons than because I understand the answer to that question."

"Well, I cannot believe in Christ without an answer to my question," Faust continued. "But perhaps we do have a creator. If so, then our lives must have divine meaning, but the problem is in discovering that meaning. Let us begin with what we know. We know that we act as physical bodies," Faust reflected. "So that must be part of our purpose. "

"What do you mean?" Julian asked.

"I mean part of our purpose in existing is to act as material bodies in a material universe. In this sense we are no different from stones or water. And we fulfill this purpose perfectly. Our bodies perfectly obey the physical laws which govern all matter and energy."

"Very interesting," said Julian. "I had not thought of that before. Isn't it odd how our purpose in acting as physical bodies is so different from our purpose in making choices?"

Faust shook his head in disagreement. "There is no real choice," he said. "Our brain is an organ made of matter. The laws that govern it and its so-called choices are the same as those that govern the flow of water and electricity. We are merely organic machines."

From his place by the fire, Anfortas stirred. "No," he said, "she must be right about our ability to choose. In a universe where free will did not exist, regret would not exist, and regret certainly exists in this universe."

Faust looked condescendingly at the knight. "How does the presence of regret change anything?" he asked.

"What do you think the word 'regret' means?" Anfortas asked.

"I would say that regret is sorrow for past mistakes," the philosopher returned.

"Is there a difference in the kind of sorrow that one feels for past mistakes and the kind one feels for general misfortune that is not the result of past mistakes?" Anfortas asked.

"What do you mean?" Faust asked defensively.

"I mean that a man may be sad that he was ever born, but he does not feel *regret* at having been born since the choice of being born was not his to make. Our bodies take shape and grow in the womb according to the laws that govern the physical universe. But if our every action were thus governed by these same laws, we would never recognize a distinction between the sorrow we feel for our fate and the sorrow we feel for our past choices. Nature, *or God*," he glanced sarcastically at Julian, "has been merciful enough to allow us not one but two kinds of sorrow."

"Perhaps it is merciful indeed, Anfortas," she answered softly, "that God allows us to feel regret. Regret can move us to seek him for healing."

Anfortas looked hard at Julian. "Have you ever done anything that you regret?"

Julian's voice was quiet and steady. "Of course," she answered.

"I find that hard to believe."

She returned his gaze thoughtfully. "Have you Anfortas?" she asked.

"Have I what?"

"Ever done anything that you regret?"

Anfortas looked away, and the muscles of his face grew taunt. He seemed curiously stumped for the moment, and when he finally did speak, his voice was barely audible.

"You don't know anything, woman," he said. "You are a dreamer."

"Sometimes," Julian said, watching the knight closely, "God speaks through our dreams." But the knight uttered no word in response, nor did he move other than simply to drop his gaze to the floor and shake his head.

Eventually, Julian turned back to Faust.

"Anfortas is right, you know," she said. "What function would regret have in a universe without choice?"[xxi]

"Let us leave that aside for a moment," the professor said hastily. He seemed uncomfortable. "I have another question."

Julian waited.

"How do you explain the presence of evil?" he asked.

"Do you believe in such a thing as evil?" she asked in return.

Faust shuddered. "Oh yes," he replied.

"What is 'evil'?" she continued.

"'Evil' is *that which ought not to be*," Faust said with a haunted expression.

"If you believe in *that which ought not to be,* then you must also believe in *that which ought to be,* which is goodness."

After a moment's reflection, he reluctantly nodded in agreement.

"If you believe in goodness, then you must also believe in a Creator. Why, then, do you still speak of God's existence hypothetically?"

"Because," Faust said, "a man may be good and not believe in God."

"I do not deny that an atheist may love virtue and do good things, but this love of virtue and goodness contradicts his atheism, for if he believes in goodness, in *what ought to be,* then he should also believe in a Creator since to say that something *ought to be* a certain way is to imply that it has a purpose in existing. If a creation does not fulfill its purpose, it *is not* as it *ought to be.* But an uncreated thing simply *is.* It makes no sense to say that it *ought to be* a certain way. If an atheist feels an inner prompting to behave in a particular way, if his heart tells him that he ought to be humble, patient, kind, forgiving, and faithful, then he should ask himself where that prompting comes from, for such a prompting should not exist in an uncreated heart."

"I fear you are avoiding the question, Julian," Faust interrupted. "I ask you again: how do you explain the presence of evil. How do you answer Epicurus's old questions: 'Is God willing to prevent evil, but not able? Then he is impotent. Is he able, but not willing? Then is he malevolent. Is he both able and willing? Whence then is evil?'"[xxii]

Julian did not answer right away, and I took this to mean that she was unsure of what to say. Wanting to help, I attempted to contribute to the discussion. "Evil only 'exists' negatively, as the absence of goodness," I said. "It is insubstantial and has no real existence,[xxiii] like darkness. There is no such thing as darkness, only light."

Anfortas looked up at me with an angry scowl. "Only an idiot would sit in a dark room and babble on about how there is no such thing as darkness."

I flared against him indignantly. "In philosophy you must be very careful of your definitions. Evil can be defined as the absence of goodness, just as darkness is defined as the absence of light. Goodness can exist without evil, but evil cannot exist without goodness. Of course, I'm not saying that evil things do not happen. I'm simply saying that evil does not have positive existence."

Anfortas's eyes narrowed. He sat up with calculated slowness and leaned menacingly toward me.

"'I can prove that evil exists," he said, and a wicked grin played across his face in the firelight, "but I won't be using definitions."

"Anfortas," Julian said and gently held her thin hand out to restrain him.

"Who appointed you as my watchdog?" he growled. Autumn jumped up from my side, running to her mistress, but Julian held her other hand out to the little girl reassuringly.

"Anfortas," the elderly woman addressed the knight again, this time more firmly. "We are condemned here together. He is only trying to understand, just like you and me." I thought Anfortas might say something in response, but, after a tense moment, he simply rolled over to face the fireplace, reclining on his elbow once again.

"I agree with you in principle," she told me with a smile. "But, Johann," she said, turning to the scholar, "if you are asking me why God allows evil things to happen to the innocent, I confess that I do not know the answer to that question. I do believe, however, that all will be well with those innocent ones. God suffers with them, though he is Innocence itself, and by his suffering all will be healed of evil: 'He was wounded for our transgressions, He was bruised for our iniquities; the chastisement for our peace was upon Him, and by His stripes we are healed.'[xxiv]

If, on the other hand, you are asking me how *that which ought not to be* ever comes to be, I believe that evil is among us as a consequence of our own poor choices and those of others. Part of God's will for creatures like us is that we be allowed to choose. This allows for the possibility of death and evil if our choices are contrary to God's will. Each choice we make results in either the life or death of some aspect of our nature, depending upon whether or not that choice is in accord with God's will.

Of course, I do not believe that every decision is a moral one," she clarified, "simply that each decision leads to the life or death of some aspect of our nature. If the choice involves a moral decision, then it will lead to the life or death of our soul. If the decision is not moral, then it will lead to the life or death of something else. For instance, if Thales the philosopher had broken his neck and died when he fell into a well because he chose to watch the stars rather than his feet, the resulting death would not have been of his soul, only of his physical body."

Faust managed the slightest smile in response to this example, which Julian had obviously intended to lighten the mood, but its appeal was lost on me. Autumn sat quietly beside Julian; I missed the feel of her little body at my side. While she had been with me, held close in my arms, I could pretend to assume some of her innocence and natural affection, which seemed to render her impervious to the horror of her doom. Now, however, she was away, and my thoughts turned bitterly to Anfortas, whose rude outburst had robbed me of her consolation. Ironically, I soon found that the growing hatred I felt for the knight brought a perversely pleasant distraction of its own. As I stared at his recumbent form outlined by the red glow of the fireplace, I rehearsed the various ways that I should have responded to his threat.

He would not threaten me again unanswered.

Five

Meanwhile, Faust continued the debate. "Can we then conclude that our lives are completely in our own hands?" he asked. "If only we made all the right choices, would we live forever?"

"I don't think so, for two reasons," Julian said. "First, every other creature with the ability to choose would also have to make perfect decisions. That doesn't seem very likely, and the wrong decisions of others can hurt us. But in addition to this, I believe that all of creation is condemned to death and that there is no way we can overcome that condemnation on our own."

"You say that because you are a Christian, Julian," said Faust.

Julian shrugged. "Have you ever known anyone or anything to overcome death?"

"No."

"Why do you suppose that is?" she asked.

"I don't know why; I only know that it is so," he said a little defensively. "Perhaps death is natural, like birth. Perhaps we shouldn't try or desire to overcome it. Doesn't your own George MacDonald say, 'How strange this fear of death is! We are never frightened at a sunset'?"[xxv]

"Are you not afraid of death, Faust?" Julian asked.

"Do you think George MacDonald was?" he challenged.

"Perhaps he was less afraid than most, but those who regard such a sunset without fear, do so in proportion to their belief in a coming dawn. They believe in One who has overcome death for their sake."

"George MacDonald is dead," Faust replied flatly.

"And by the mercy of God, he will live again," answered Julian. "But this does not mean that death is natural. Leaving aside the consideration of Christ, do you agree that every living thing in nature desires to overcome death, and that no living thing actually succeeds in overcoming it?"

"Yes," he admitted. "Everything that lives seeks to maintain its life. Our bodies testify that this is so. Everything about them is designed by Nature either to maintain our own life or to engender new life. Each thing that lives in the universe desires continued life, primarily as an individual but also collectively as a species. I believe any biologist would agree with this. Life is important. In fact, it is of the utmost importance, and its preservation seems to be the focus of all living things in nature. But you are right; the point you bring up is one I don't deny. Why is it that the one thing (eternal life) toward which all living beings direct all their energies is never attained by them? What a bizarre condition. Death overtakes everything eventually. Why? It does not make sense to me that death would be natural, and yet that Nature should fight so strongly, and so impotently, against it.

Now Julian, don't misunderstand me. I'm aware of the Christian explanation for all of this - that death is *not* the natural state of things, that it entered the universe through the sin, or bad choice, of Adam, and that all of creation has been groaning for the redemption of its failing life ever since. I'm not discounting that explanation. I simply have no precise reasons to accept it. I will grant, however, that death is as inevitable as it is unnatural and that all living creatures desire life."

Julian digested this for a space and nodded her head. Then, unexpectedly, Anfortas spoke up again, though he kept his back to the group. "Why do you grant that?" he asked.

Faust hesitated. "Grant what?" he asked.

"That all living creatures desire life."

"Because all the evidence that I can glean suggests that that is true," Faust responded.

"You're wrong," Anfortas answered.

"Why do you say that?" The scholar looked puzzled, but Anfortas did not answer immediately. After a long moment of stillness, he turned around to face Faust.

"What about suicides?" he asked.

"Suicides are an aberration," Faust responded, dismissing the question.

Julian, however, looked back at Anfortas and regarded him curiously before speaking. "I don't believe anyone wants to die," she said kindly, "not even people who kill themselves. I think they only want to be free of their pain, not their lives."

Anfortas said nothing. He only shifted slightly, making it impossible to see his expression because of the shadows.

"The soul of a person may die long before his body does," Julian said quietly. "Our souls die by our own evil choices, but Christ offers life to our whole being, not simply our bodies."

From where he sat, Faust cleared his throat. Evidently, he expected an imminent departure into Christian dogma, but he did not call Julian to task for it, perhaps because he had no alternative to offer at the moment.

Reluctantly, Julian looked down at Autumn, who was leaning against her comfortably. "Everyone will be marred by evil. Everyone," she said, brushing the little girl's hair with her sensitive fingers. "It's an abomination far worse than the death of our bodies. No amount of trying to be good will keep evil at bay. Ask those who try hardest, and I believe they will be the quickest to admit that. Gandhi longed for purity, but even such a great soul as his feared that he would die with this longing unfulfilled, despite continual and strenuous efforts to realize it. He prayed without ceasing that some great spirit, moved by divine pity, might be born among us to deliver us from our own sin.[xxvi] And Saint Paul expressed something similar when he wrote, 'The good that I will to do, I do not do; but the evil I will not to do, that I practice. O wretched man that I am! Who will deliver me from this body of death? I thank God-through Jesus Christ our

Lord!'[xxvii] Death is the sign of a broken universe rather than the natural state of creation. But Christ is that great spirit, fired with divine pity, who died in our place so that we could escape from death. If we trust in his love and forgiveness, he will give us eternal life."

"Is that why you try to be good," mocked Anfortas from the shadows. "Is that why you love, so you can go to heaven?"

Julian did not answer immediately.

"And what is the point of being good if all the rest of humanity is evil and faithless?" he pressed.

"Do good out of gratitude toward God for your life," she answered. "Do it out of love for him, or do it for yourself, if nothing else. You don't have to be a Christian to realize that nothing in life is more important or satisfying than love. *God is Love.* Love and forgiveness *are life.* Is it a mere coincidence that they are also the heart of Christianity? I believe people ultimately desire these things, which are the life of the soul, even more than they desire the life of the body. Christ offers them to us, and I believe we should try to follow his example by offering them to one another."

"If I may," Faust interjected. "I appreciate your thoughts, Julian, but I'm afraid your conclusions are based on premises that I don't quite accept. You speak of the soul, for instance, but what is that? How could it live or die?"

"Your soul is your self," Julian replied. She sighed as she tried to think of a better way to express herself. In the midst of this she turned her gaze toward me. "Have you ever considered the fact that you exist?" she asked me. I blinked in confusion, not knowing whether or not she wanted me to answer. It was strange that she should address me when Faust had asked the question.

"I'm not asking whether you have considered the fact that your unique body exists. That could have been predicted and explained by a geneticist. I mean have you considered the fact that *you* exist, that it is *you* and nobody else looking out of those eyes?" I shifted uncomfortably, and her own eyes looked straight into me as she continued to speak. "Have you ever considered that, of all the creatures who have ever lived, or who are living now, or who will live, *this* one," she pointed at me, pausing the length of a breath, "is *you*?"

After she finished, she continued to watch me for the space of another breath before turning again to Faust. "Anyway, that is how I have always thought about the soul," she said. Faust nodded, but I could tell from his expression that he was not satisfied.

"Perhaps we should return to the original objective of our discussion, which is to determine whether or not we should follow Christ. Now, Julian," he said, "can you provide some rational line of reasoning, some proof that Christ was God, as he claimed?"

Julian looked down at Autumn again and continued brushing the little girl's hair with her fingers as she tried to think of a way to answer Faust.

"What is the point of asking that?" Anfortas spoke up sharply. "You want her to prove that Christ was God? Think how absurd your question is," the knight laughed scornfully. "Christ was a man, nothing more, a naïve man who was betrayed and murdered. He died. Can God die? Wouldn't that make him imperfect?" He did not wait for Julian to answer. "I have a much better question. If God exists, then why does he keep himself so far from us that he may as well *not* exist? Why conceal himself? Why would the great I AM make it so hard to believe that HE IS when he could just as easily talk to me, face to face? Why isn't his existence the most obvious, self-evident fact of our lives?"

"He is never far from us, Anfortas. He is closer than the breath in our lungs, but he does not want to overwhelm us with the splendor of his presence because such splendor would compel us, of necessity, to love and worship him. He desires, rather, for us to choose to love him of our own free will; therefore, he conceals his full majesty and woos us by subtle methods, giving hints of his presence everywhere in the hope that we will seek him out. Hence the proverb: 'It is the glory of God to conceal a matter, and to search out a matter is the glory of kings.'"

"And how does one search out the matter of Christ?"

"By faithful obedience. Christ has said, 'If you love me, keep my commandments. I will not leave you orphans; I will come to you. He who has my commandments and keeps them, it is he who loves me. And he who loves me will be loved by my father, and I will love him, *and manifest myself to him.*'[xxviii] I think the surest way to know Christ is to follow him, to do our best to obey his commands."

"And what are they?" asked Anfortas.

"Love the LORD your God with all your heart, with all your soul, with all your strength and with all your mind, and your neighbor as yourself,"[xxix] she answered.

"This is the divine purpose of our existence. I believe if we do this we will come to understand that Christ truly is who he claimed to be, and we will know this in a more profound way than we could ever understand by simply arranging arguments to prove his claim logically.

Maybe this is why Jesus was so fond of parables," she continued. "A parable conceals the truth of a lesson in such a way that purely intellectual attempts to understand it often fail where even a child could understand by simply practicing its lesson faithfully. Jesus said, 'Therefore I speak to them in parables, because seeing they do not see, and hearing they do not hear, nor do they understand. And in them the prophecy of Isaiah is fulfilled, which says: "Hearing you will hear and shall not understand."'[xxx] Have you ever noticed how often people had trouble understanding his parables? And he rarely explained them. Maybe all of life is a parable from God that we will never understand unless we try to follow Jesus's example and practice love faithfully."

Anfortas slowly drew his breath in and grimaced, his eyes half closed. "I believe Christ *himself* practiced what he preached. I believe he forgave, I believe he loved, I believe he trusted," the knight's voice trembled, rising in pitch as he continued, "and I believe he perfectly manifests the end result of such foolishness: betrayal, and a shameful, agonizing death. Why do you continue to ignore that fact? I find it amusing that you talk about a child's understanding. Isn't it obvious that Christ's views were indeed those of a child, a naïve child who had no understanding of reality? And so are yours, Julian, the views of a child. Are you just afraid to understand how the world really works? Is that it? *'When I was a child, I thought as a child,'''* he smiled sarcastically, *"'but when I became a man, I put away childish things.'*[xxxi] You would do well to do the same."

Julian patiently received what he had to say, letting her eyes drop quietly to the upturned face of Autumn. "There is evil in the world, Anfortas, in all of us, and we constantly hurt one another with it. I have never said otherwise."

"Where is God then?" Anforas asked harshly.

"Christ asked the same question on the cross.[xxxii] Ask him for the answer, but ask as a child," she replied.

The expression on Anfortas's face was one of angry frustration as he and Julian stared at one another silently.

Then Faust spoke up. "If God's essential nature is mercy and love, then how do you explain hell? How could a God of mercy and love create a place of *infinite* torture for those of his creatures who disobey him?"

By the quiver in his voice, I could tell that this topic had particular significance to him.

"I asked him that very question myself once," Julian said.

"Asked who?" Faust frowned in puzzlement.

"God."

"Ah," Faust said condescendingly.

"He told me that I would see for myself that everything would be all right, but I found his words hard to believe because the Christian faith rests on God's word, and from that word we learn that, while the believers will be saved, many creatures, angels and humans, will be damned. How then would everything be all right as God had told me? His only answer was to remind me that what is impossible for me is not impossible for God, and then I remembered that he had said the same thing to his disciples once."[xxxiii]

"When?" asked Faust.

"In the gospel of Mark, although he was speaking of heaven, not hell. He told the disciples that it is harder for a rich man to enter heaven than for a camel to go through the eye of a needle. His disciples were astounded by this and said to one another, 'Who then can be saved?' But looking at them, Jesus said, 'With men it is impossible, but not with God.'"xxxiv

"I have heard," countered Faust, "that 'the eye of a needle' was the name of a city gate in Jerusalem through which a camel could pass if it pushed very hard. In that case, the Christ of the gospel is not using the word 'impossible' as the Christ in your vision was."

"That is why I do not believe he was referring to an actual gate in the city. If he was, why were the disciples so astounded at the saying? It does not astound me that a camel can push its way through a city gate if it tries hard enough, and I do not believe it would have astounded the disciples either. Christ must have meant that it is as possible for a rich person to enter heaven as it is for a camel to go through the eye of a needle. In other words, it is impossible. The disciples understood this, hence their astonishment and fear that nobody would be saved."

This did not comfort Faust in the least as he fidgeted with the gold chain hanging from his neck.

"But Christ goes on to say that, for God, all things are possible," Julian continued. "This is why I believe that all will be well in spite of the fact that this seems impossible in light of the reality of hell. God is love. Trust in him, Johann," she urged.

"So, you have no answer again," Faust said wryly. "Such mysticism is antithetical to rational thought. I refuse to accept it, and I challenge the idea of a God who expects me to renounce my capacity for reason."

I waited for Julian to say something more, but she was quiet. I became anxious for the sake of the debate and began trying to think of a rebuttal to the great scholar, but, before I could arrange my thoughts, Anfortas spoke up. My stomach turned at the sound of his voice.

"Why do you put so much faith in the Bible, Julian?" he baited her.

"I believe God has taken special care to speak to us through the Bible. It is his Word. It is sacred."

"What about all the other books in the world, religious or otherwise? Does God speak through them as well?"

"He may. God is Truth. Whatever is true in other books is also from God, but I believe that God has most closely directed the creation of the Bible because it tells the story of Christ."

"What about the Old Testament?" he retorted.

"That too is the story of Christ," she answered. "It prophetically foreshadows his coming, the coming of the stone that was cut by no human hands, which grew into a mighty mountain and filled the whole earth."[xxxv]

"Christians are notoriously poor interpreters of such prophecies," Anfortas said. "Behold, the virgin shall conceive and bear a son,"[xxxvi] he quoted from memory. "Matthew takes this line from Isaiah and applies it to the virgin birth of Christ, but the Hebrew word that Isaiah uses for the woman who will bear this child is *almâh*, which simply means 'young woman,' not 'virgin;' it has no reference to whether or not she has had sex, only to the fact that she is of marriageable age. If Isaiah had meant to indicate that the woman would be an actual virgin, he would have used the word *běthulâ*. Matthew must have read the passage in the Septuagint, the Greek translation of the Old Testament, and concluded that the Messiah would be born of a virgin. The Septuagint mistakenly translates the Hebrew word *almâh* as *parthenos*, which does mean virgin."

"So, you think that the Septuagint accurately predicted that the Messiah would be born of a virgin?" Julian asked hopefully.

Anfortas paused. "No," he said hesitantly. "No, you are missing the point. Isaiah told Ahaz, 'The Lord Himself will give you a sign: Behold, the young woman shall conceive and bear a son, and shall call his name Immanuel. Curds and honey he shall eat, that he may know to refuse the evil and choose the good. For before the child shall know to refuse the evil and choose the good, the land that you dread will be forsaken by both her kings.' [xxxvii] The sign is that a young woman would have a son, and that while this boy was still a child (before he knew to choose good over evil and while he was still eating milk and honey) the power of the two kings whom Ahaz feared would be broken. My point is that this sign was meant for Ahaz. Therefore, it must describe something that happened in Ahaz's lifetime, not the birth of Christ, which happened 700 years later. But Matthew misreads this and ignorantly applies it to Christ."

"Why would the Hebrew translators of the Septuagint have chosen the word *parthenos* if they did not think the word *almâh* meant 'virgin'?" Julian asked.

Anfortas shrugged. "I assume they *did* think it meant virgin. They made a mistake, one which Matthew repeated."

"I wonder," Julian said. "Even if the Septuagint translators mistakenly believed that this Immanuel who was born in Ahaz's lifetime was born of a virgin, they were correct to use the term *parthenos* in a passage that would later signify Mary, the virgin mother of Christ. And one thing is clear to me: Matthew did not make a mistake in applying this passage to Mary and Christ."

"How could you believe that the Septuagint translators made a mistake in translation and yet not believe that Matthew also made a mistake when he agreed with that translation?"

"Matthew was aware of what he was doing. He, like the translators of the Septuagint, knew that the prophecy applied to a boy in Ahaz's own day. How could he not? It is obvious on the first reading of the passage. But he also knew the history of Christ, and he knew that the passage as it stood in the Septuagint applied to Christ, regardless of whether or not the translators of the Septuagint made a mistake. God works through humans, and he often uses even our mistakes for our benefit."

"I had thought you more honest than this, Julian. You are going well out of your way simply to cover up Matthew's blunder."

This last comment outraged me; that he should thus insult her integrity was unpardonable. Julian, however, said nothing in her own defense.

"I must admit," Faust added. "Christ and his disciples do seem to have taken liberties with many of the passages considered to be 'Messianic' by the Jews of his time. Like most prophesies, they could have been interpreted to apply to many people, as, indeed, they often were. More people than Jesus claimed to be the Messiah."

"But that doesn't make his own claim invalid," Julian said.

"No, not necessarily," Faust admitted. "But he did not just claim to be the Messiah. He claimed to be God himself."

"Didn't the Jews expect that of the Messiah - that he would be God incarnate?" Julian asked. "Another of the prophesies which came to be associated with the expected Messiah even before the time of Christ is also in the book of Isaiah: 'For unto us a child is born, unto us a son is given. And his name will be called Wonderful, Counselor, *Mighty God, Everlasting Father*, Prince of Peace.'"[xxxviii]

"That also has nothing to do with Christ," replied Anfortas. "Isaiah is talking about King Hezekiah. As for his being called 'Mighty God' and 'Everlasting Father,' many ancient Hebrews were given names like that. The name 'Hezekiah' itself means, 'God is strong'."

"Perhaps King Hezekiah was a sort of foreshadowing of the true Messiah, like you have foreshadowing in a story, except that this story is written in the ink of reality by the finger of God," Julian suggested.

Faust smiled slightly. "That is a very poetic view, Julian, but not a well reasoned one," he said.

"Haven't you got something better to try to deceive us with?" Anfortas followed up.

I could stand no more.

"What about his other name?" I asked, my voice shaking with adrenaline and anger. It was my first attempt to join the debate since my earlier contribution on the nature of good and evil. Everyone was somewhat surprised to hear me speak, and I must admit that my own voice sounded out of place even to me.

"What other name?" Anfortas asked dryly.

My bitterness against the young knight swelled like an infection. "The name in the very passage of Isaiah that you brought up a moment ago," I said. My words were slow and deliberate in an attempt to sound condescending. He seemed to realize my intention and laughed.

"Go on," he urged.

"The prophecy says, 'Behold, the virgin shall conceive and bear a son, and shall call his name *Immanuel*,'" I said. "This name, which means 'God be with you,' clearly reflects the divine nature of Christ."

He laughed again, even louder.

"What are you laughing at, you hyena?" I snapped irritably.

Out of the corner of my eye, I saw Julian sigh.

"Well, in the first place," he began, "*Immanuel* means 'God with us,' not 'God be with you.'" As he said this, I remembered that that is so and felt my face flush with embarrassment and anger. "I would have thought someone so finicky about his definitions wouldn't have made such a ridiculous blunder, and I mean ridiculous in its purest denotation, being from the Latin *ridere*, a second conjugation verb meaning 'to laugh at.'" He paused to relish my humiliation before continuing. "In the second place, that example is as weak as the one Julian just came up with, and for the same reasons. All these Biblical explanations are nothing more than delusional constructs at best. At worst, they are simply lies."

"Which are you calling me," I asked, "a liar or a madman?"

"You pick," he said.

"Both of you quiet down," Julian said firmly. She spoke quickly, apparently hoping to pacify the situation by taking the lead again. "Between the two of you, I have learned another reason for thinking that Christ was God," she said. "It occurs to me that anyone who claims to be God is either a liar, a madman, or God.[xxxix] I disagree with you, Anfortas. I believe the Jewish nation was expecting a Messiah at the time of Christ's birth. And I believe that the Scriptures indicate that this Messiah would be God himself, in the form of a human. So, I don't think Christ's claim to divinity was simply a construct of his disciples. He claimed to be the Messiah, which is to say he claimed to be God. And he claimed to be the God of the Hebrews, the self-existing Creator, greater than his creation and separate from it, not the sort of god that pantheists believe in."

"What is a pantheist?" I asked.

"I think pantheists believe that God and the universe are synonymous. So when a pantheist says, 'I am God,' it carries a completely different meaning than when Christ claimed to be God. If any of us met someone who claimed to be God in the sense that Christ meant, we would consider him either to be a liar or mad."

"I'm perfectly content to believe that Christ was a madman," said Anfortas.

"Shut up," I said.

Julian gave me a reproving look, which stung a little. Why did she put up with him? And why rebuke *me*? For her sake I held my tongue, but my anger against the knight seethed, and I clenched my fists until I thought blood would spurt from my nails.

"I wonder," Faust spoke up, "if there is not another option besides liar or madman. From what we can read of him, I think it is safe to conclude that Christ was not a liar. But he needn't be a madman either, I think. Perhaps he was simply mistaken. An honest man may hold false opinions and yet not be a liar or mad."

"I agree," said Julian, "but not the opinion that he is God. No sane, honest man would claim such a thing unless it were true."

"I have to disagree," he said.

"Have you ever known anyone who claimed to be God?" she asked.

"No," he said.

"Then that is why you disagree," said Julian. "I have met several people who believed they were God. All were insane. If you had ever met one of them you would notice immediately the difference between their behavior and that of Christ. Where Christ was humble, they are arrogant and self-indulgent, where Christ resisted Satan's temptation to rule the nations of the world, they suffer from delusions of grandeur and megalomania, where Christ, for love of us, bore insults and torture without a word of protest, they howl indignantly at the slightest offence. From what we know of Christ you say that he wasn't a liar. I agree. And from what I know of madmen, I say Christ was not mad, yet he claimed to be God."

While Faust and Julian were talking, Anfortas and I had held each other's gaze without wavering. I glared fiercely at the knight as my anger came to a head. I couldn't stand him. I didn't deserve to be there with him. I didn't deserve to be there at all.

Then Anfortas's face grew oddly resigned and emotionless. He blinked lazily, once, and then rolled over to face the fire.

Something about this last act of his struck me as so dismissive, so flagrant an insult, that I felt I could no longer contain myself. With a roar, I leapt to my feet and charged him. Autumn scrambled to get out of my path, and Julian held up her arm reflexively. I remember that she yelled something at me, but I could no more hear her over the wildness in my brain than if she were screaming into a storm.

The short space between the knight and myself evaporated quickly, and yet I knew he had time to anticipate my coming. He could have done something to prepare for it, but he did not so much as flinch as I came crashing into him from behind. I remember, even in my rage, thinking how strange that was.

The force of my impact sent us both skidding across the stone floor, almost into the fireplace itself. I remember feeling the knight's mailed throat under my fingers, and I remember pounding my fist into his upturned face, but I also remember that none of my blows carried any force. The harder I swung, the less effective they seemed to be. Any second I expected him to use his greater strength and martial skill to throw me off and attack, but he did nothing to fight back or even defend himself. Before long, this bizarre, unexpected behavior of his compelled me to stop my assault, out of breath and bewildered.

And Anfortas began to weep.

At first all I could do was stare stupidly at him. His eyes were closed and tears wet his face, drawn tight now with anguish. I stood up slowly and staggered back a few steps, still panting from exertion. The residual adrenaline in my legs made them tremble, and I stood uncertainly in the shadows. I didn't understand. Julian and Faust watched in shocked silence as his sobs grew louder and louder, echoing miserably off the walls of the great hall. I continued to stare at the knight in disbelief. There was not a single mark on his face. I didn't understand. I wanted to ask him what was wrong, but I said nothing, seeing that the question would have been absurd coming from me at that moment.

Julian moved first. She arose with some difficulty due to her age and walked slowly to where Anfortas lay weeping. Then, leaning heavily on her knees, she sat down beside the young knight with a soft grunt of effort.

"Anfortas," she said gently and touched his shoulder.

He reached blindly for her.

"I'm here. I'm right here," she said, leaning over him as if to gather up a child. As she embraced him his body began to convulse in rhythmic spasms of sorrow, and a pitifully low moan sounded from his throat.

Then he lost himself entirely. He buried his face violently into Julian's neck and clung to her so fiercely that he seemed to be attacking her. Terrible, shuddering wails muffled themselves against her sympathetic body. It was a lonely wailing, a horrible, fearful wailing that seemed to feed on its own strength. What had I done?

Then I noticed little Autumn. I don't know how I had missed it before, but she too was crying. She clutched the *lapsit exillis* and stood near her mistress, looking up at her for comfort. Her own crying echoed that of Anfortas as each of the knight's wails heightened the intensity of Autumn's distress. Immediately, I ached to comfort her and moved toward the little girl, intending to hold her since Julian could not. But when Autumn saw me coming, she screamed in terror and frantically pressed herself closer to Julian. I stopped. A sick feeling of shame began to rise in my stomach. I looked left at Faust, hoping for sympathy or justification for what I had done, but his face was as blank and stupid as I imagined my own must have been. Reluctantly, I turned to Julian, fearful of her condemnation, but she was too occupied with Anfortas and Autumn to take note of me. She winced with pain at the tightness of the knight's embrace as she rocked back and forth speaking gently to him and Autumn, both of whom she now cradled awkwardly as best she could.

Suddenly I felt completely alone. Waves of self-pity and regret began to rise and swallow me in their cold wake. I wanted someone to hold on to, someone to hold on to me, but there was nobody.

"Anfortas," I said. My voice wavered, and I too began to cry. "Anfortas, I'm sorry." I moved closer and knelt beside him. "Anfortas, please. I'm sorry," I said, reaching out to touch his back, but he would not look up. "Anfortas," I continued, but Julian shook her head and indicated that I should let him be. "I'm sorry," I pleaded one last time.

Despair finally overwhelmed me. *Death would be welcome*, I thought to myself. Mechanically, I stood up and walked away. Nobody spoke to me. The debate was over. It was replaced by a foreboding sense of dread, which seemed to brood over everything now. Anfortas had stopped crying but still clung wearily to Julian like the lone survivor of a shipwreck clinging to a bit of flotsam. Autumn whimpered quietly. Julian spoke in her soft, reassuring voice to the child and the knight, but these were the only sounds in the cavernous hall as I slumped against the wall and slid to the floor, hugging my knees close to my chest.

Six

Complete silence eventually enveloped everything as each person wandered alone in the labyrinth of his or her own thoughts. There seemed nothing left to do but wait, and the wait was agony. On the opposite side of our cell loomed the great metal doors like grim sentinels. For a long time I watched the massive things tensely as if they were alive, waiting for them to speak or move, and for a long time they did neither.

But finally they did.

The long expected noise of the great doors' heavy bolt being thrown back slammed into the fragile silence of the hall with such strength that Faust let out an involuntary yelp of fear. It was real. It was happening. Again, my heart began to beat frantically. Who would be taken? Would they come for more than one of us at a time? Surely it would not be me. I had been the last one in.

The huge doors swung outward on their metallic hinges, and there, obscured by shadow, stood the executioner.   At the sight of him, I began to shake uncontrollably. My breathing came in quick gasps. "Oh dear God, please not me," I begged. "Please don't let him take me."

The executioner stood on the threshold briefly and swept his gaze across all of us. He was completely cloaked in black so that nothing of his body could be seen. His hands were gauntleted, and a voluminous robe reached down to heavy boots. Only darkness appeared to stare out from the recesses of his deep cowl as he thoroughly surveyed the entire group. At last his unseen eyes came to rest upon me. I froze. Then, with terrible deliberateness, he began to walk across the hall toward me.

"No," I said, gasping for breath. I felt sick. My teeth began to chatter, and I clamped them shut to keep from vomiting. "No," I said again, shaking my head pleadingly.

"NO!" I screamed it this time and surged upward with my back against the hard wall. "I was just brought here! Why me? Why are you taking me? What have I done?"

But he gave no answer. He simply continued his unhurried, inexorable approach. I felt desperate and looked wildly over toward the little group. Faust was so frightened that he could only cover his face mutely and tremble. I looked to Julian, but she seemed, finally, not to know how to offer comfort. Her mouth opened helplessly, and from her eyes I could tell that she was afraid too.

I was alone, completely alone. And I was going to die. No one could help me. No one could save me. I turned again toward the executioner. He was halfway across the room now, and the methodical clump of his boots grew louder and louder. His robe whispered ominously with the slow, steady rhythm of his motion. I began to shake more violently and sank again to my knees, covering my face. Footstep after footstep fell, each upon another, and that upon another, and that upon another, until I thought I would go mad.

Then, suddenly, a different sound came to my ears.

"Larry..."

I looked up, terrified.

There, standing beside Julian, was Anfortas. He stared at me for a moment as if in doubt, his wide blue eyes reflecting a strange, intense sincerity such as I could not have imagined in his expression before. We regarded one another silently as the executioner's footsteps fell dreadfully closer, closer. Then the young knight nodded his head toward me in encouragement.

"God be with you," he said softly.

I hope my own expression conveyed the gratitude I felt. I couldn't speak. In that instant I felt the hard grip of the executioner on my arm. I turned, and blackness enveloped me.

Seven

The dawn entered through my ears and skin first. I was lying on sand and could hear the steady breathing of the morning tide as it broke upon the shore. I realized that I was on the beach but as yet resisted the impulse to open my eyes. The sound of gulls and terns was all around me, and I could feel the first rays of sunlight spilling over the rim of the world. It tickled to feel the moistened sand drying on my cheek and chin.

When I finally did open my eyes, it was the sun that first captured my attention. A living radiance ran merrily across the ocean surface as if in invitation to wake and dance and play with it. Stiffly, I sat up, squinting into the east, and there I saw a man standing on the shore with his back to me. Tiny wading birds stepped curiously around the hem of his black robe.

Suddenly memory, confusion, and fear all wedged themselves simultaneously into my heart. The executioner! I panicked, instinctively scrambling to my knees, but something in the executioner's behavior made me pause. *He seemed to be admiring the sunrise.* His gauntlets and boots lay beside him in the sand, and the surf lapped peacefully around his bare feet, which were like fine brass.

"I see you are awake now," he said.

I knew that voice. "Amicus!" I exclaimed in disbelief.

He smiled in acknowledgment as he turned around and lifted back the hood of his robe.

I was stunned beyond words at the unexpected sight of my friend. Nevertheless, there he stood before me, dressed in black robes of death beneath the sacred benediction of a joyful dawn. Quietly, he walked over and knelt beside me. His benevolent face shone with affection as he reached out to me. I hugged him with all my strength and began to laugh from the mingled swirl of relief and joy that danced uncontrollably in my soul.

"I can't believe it!" I said at last.

"Can't believe what?" he asked, sitting beside me and resting his elbows on his black-clad knees.

"This!" I said, gesturing to him and the beach and my scattered books. "You! I mean, what's going on?"

For an answer he turned his eyes toward me, and I remembered the first time I had seen them.

"Do you know who I am now?" he asked.

I did.

He nodded serenely and smiled at me as one friend smiles at another. "And do you know your purpose now?"

"Yes," I answered.

"Good," he acknowledged, standing and turning toward the sea, "then come." In one swift motion, he pulled the robe off and threw it where the gauntlets and boots already lay soaked in the rising surf. A strong coastal breeze again stirred his long beard and thick mane of pure white hair. Then, with vigor he set out upon the sea once more, walking swiftly over the cold grey waves toward the living sun.

And I followed him.

"Awake, you who sleep, Arise from the dead, And Christ will give you light."

-Ephesians 5:14

Endnotes

[i] William Shakespeare, *Julius Caesar*, II ii 31: "The heavens themselves blaze forth the death of princes."

[ii] Isaiah 1:18

[iii] Rene Descartes, second Meditation in *Meditations on First Philosophy*; Saint Augustine makes the same argument centuries earlier in his *City of God*, Book 11:26.

[iv] Thomas Aquinas, *Summa Theologica*, Part 1, Question 2, First Article, Objection 3

[v] Aristotle attributes this paradox to Zeno in the sixth book of *Physics*. Its analogy to a word (and The Word) is mine.

[vi] Proverbs 3:5

[vii] Proverbs 4:7-9

[viii] Thomas Aquinas, *Summa Theologica*, Part 1, Question 21, Third Article, Objection 1. Aquinas does not believe the conclusion of this argument; he merely uses it to introduce his own counter argument, which asserts that the mercy of God is not sorrowful.

[ix] Samuel Taylor Coleridge, *Biographia Literaria,* chapter 24

[x] John 14:6

[xi] Thomas Aquinas, *Summa Theologica*, Part 1, Question 2, First Article, Objection 3

[xii] Sir Thomas Malory, *Le Morte Darthur*, The Tale of the Sangrail, Of Sir Galahad

[xiii] Dante (*Inferno* 3) describes the state of those who are in Hell. The application to those who do not believe in free will is mine.

[xiv] I have paraphrased the essential idea, which is commonly associated with William of Ockham and which is usually referred to as Ockham's razor.

[xv] Thomas Aquinas makes a similar monotheistic argument from God's perfection in *Summa Theologica*, Part 1, Question 11, Third Article.

[xvi] William Blake. *The Marriage of Heaven and Hell*, Plate 19

[xvii] In *Parzival*, the Holy Grail is described as a mysterious stone, not a cup. The term *lapsit exillis* is probably a corrupted form of the Latin phrase *lapis ex caelis*, "the stone from the heavens."

[xviii] John 1:1-4

[xix] John 8:58

xx William Blake, *Auguries of Innocence*

xxi I first came across the idea that regret is a sign that we have free will in "The Dilemma of Determinism" by William James.

xxii David Hume, *Dialogues Concerning Natural Religion*, Part 10

xxiii Julian of Norwich, *Revelations of Divine Love*, Chapter 27

xxiv Isaiah 53:5

xxv I wrote to Barbara Amell, editor of *Wingfold* (a quarterly publication about George MacDonald) in an attempt to track down the source of this quote. She replied and wrote, "To my knowledge this quote does not stem from any written source of MacDonald's [but] was first attributed to him in a 1905 obituary in *The Critic* written by Jeannette Gilder, sister of the American author and editor Richard Watson Gilder. The Gilders met MacDonald during his 1872-73 North American tour; he stayed in their home for a few days on a few occasions. She claims MacDonald said this to a clergyman who had expressed apprehension over aging, but adds nothing further."

xxvi I have paraphrased Gandhi's thoughts from two different sections (Part 3, Chapter 18, and Part 5, "Farewell") of his wonderful autobiography, *The Story of My Experiments with Truth*. The application of his thoughts to Christ is my own doing.

xxvii Romans 7:15, 24-25

xxviii John 14:15-21

xxix Luke 10:27

xxx Matthew 13:13-14

xxxi I Corinthians 13:11

xxxii Matthew 27:46: "My God, my God, why have you forsaken me?"

xxxiii Julian of Norwich, *Revelations of Divine Love*, Chapter 32

xxxiv Mark 10:25-27

xxxv Daniel 2:34-35

xxxvi Isaiah 7:14

xxxvii Isaiah 7:14-16. Here I have departed from the NKJ and translated *almâh* as "young woman," to illustrate Anfortas's argument.

xxxviii Isaiah 9:6

xxxix C.S. Lewis makes this argument in *Mere Christianity*.

www.ingramcontent.com/pod-product-compliance
Lightning Source LLC
Chambersburg PA
CBHW031326040426

42443CB00005B/231